All the Things You Can Be

El Rae Press

All The Things You Can Be
Author: Bentley Selander
Publisher: El Rae Press
Publication Date: March, 2024

ISBN: 9798883677839

Copyright © 2024 by El Rae Press

All rights reserved. No part of this publication may be reproduced, distributed, or transmitted in any form or by any means, including photocopying, recording, or other electronic or mechanical methods, without the prior written permission of the publisher, except in the case of brief quotations embodied in critical reviews and certain other noncommercial uses permitted by copyright law. For permission requests, please contact the publisher at the address below:

El Rae Press
elraepress@gmail.com
www.elraepress.com

Cover Design: Bentley Selander
Interior Design and Formatting: Bentley Selander

In a sunlit garden, there lived a bee named Buzzington. Instead of collecting nectar all day, Buzzington had a special job. He fluttered from flower to flower sharing stories about life and how emotions have power.

He buzzed around, with wings full of glee, whispering to kids,

"There's so much you can be!"

He told the little bees about all of the things they could be, feel, and see. He started with his favorite one first...

Be Adventurous

"Embark on adventures, let your spirit roam free, discover wonders, beneath every tree."

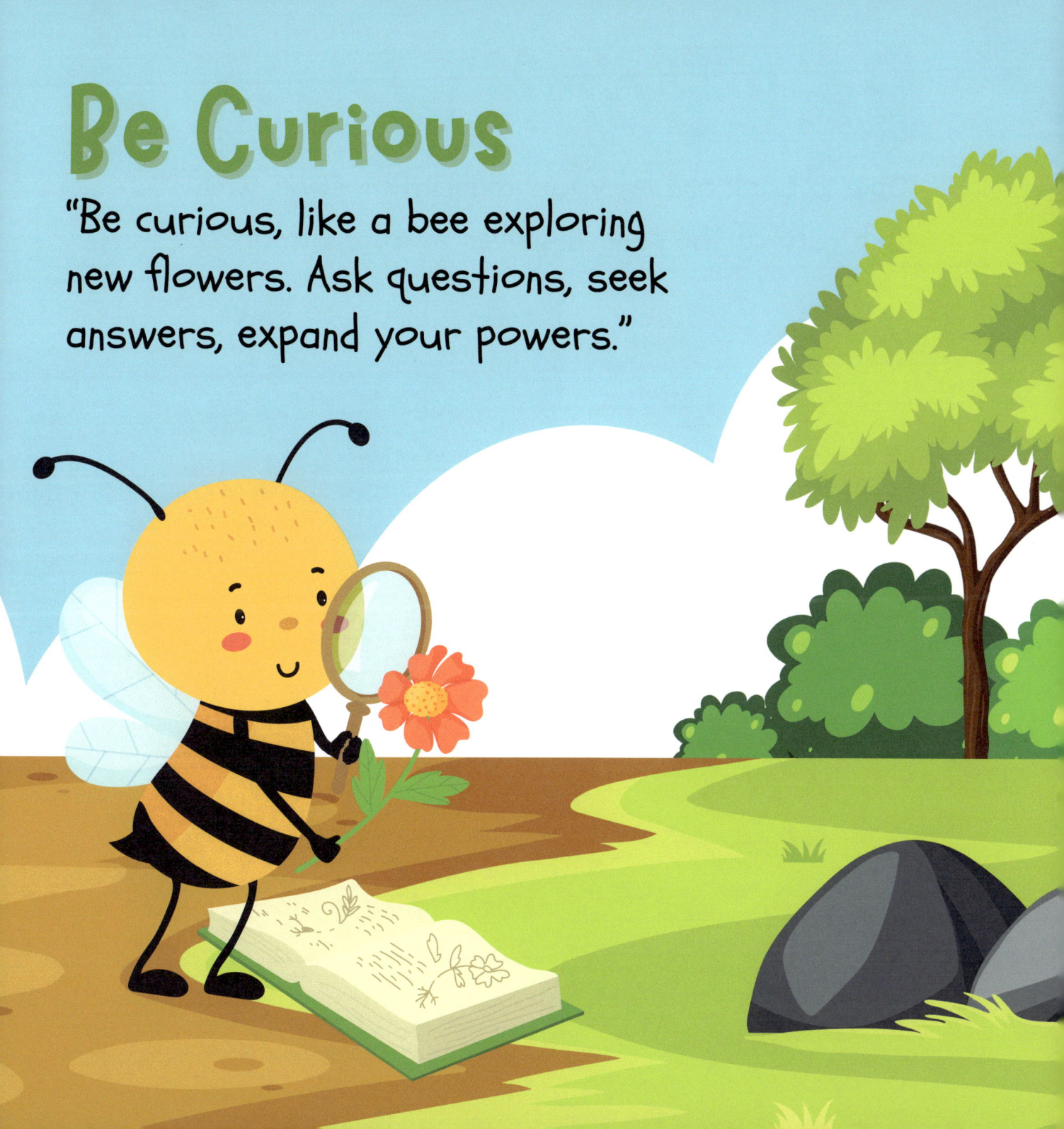

Be Curious

"Be curious, like a bee exploring new flowers. Ask questions, seek answers, expand your powers."

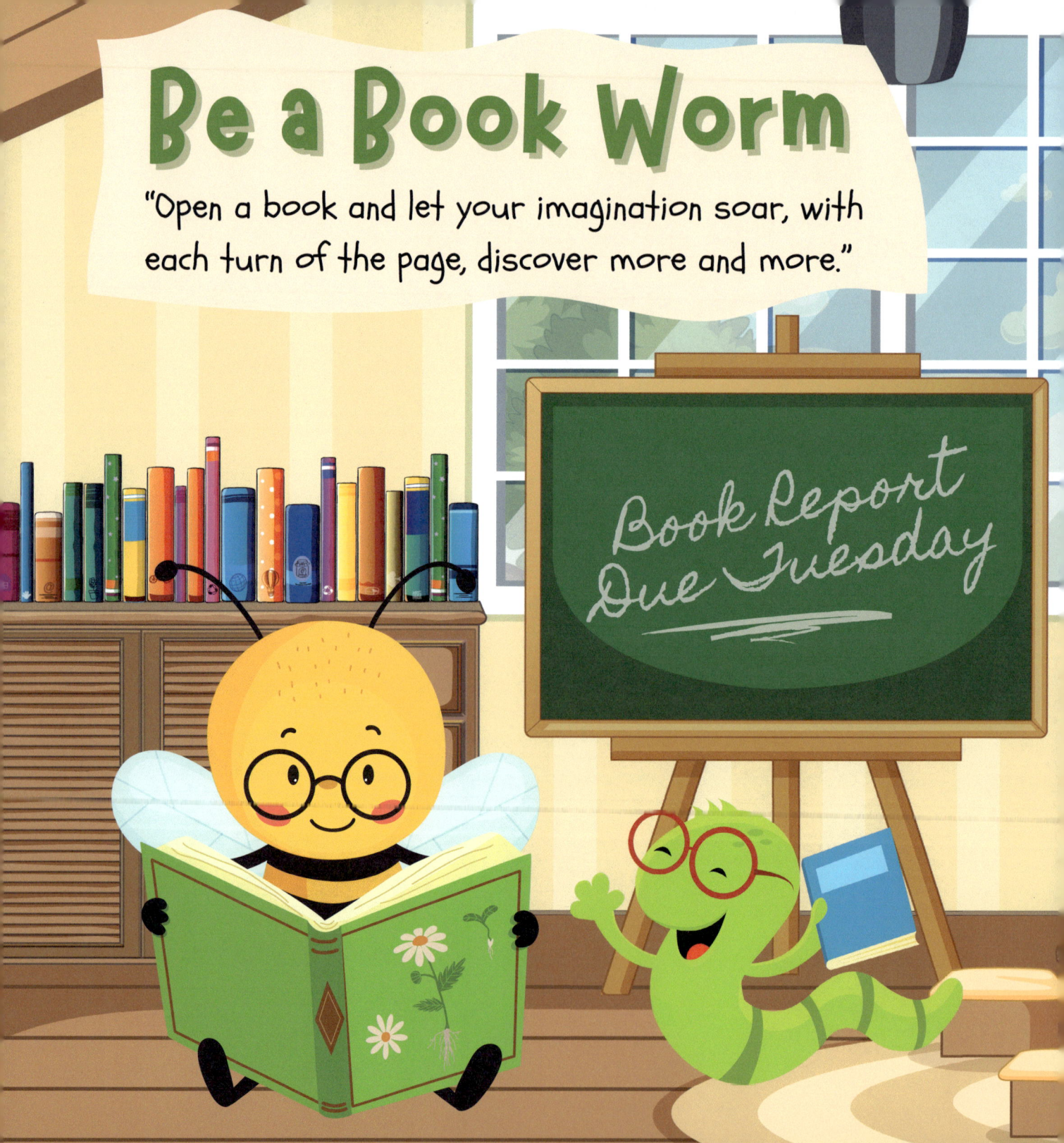

Be Cool

"Coolness isn't just about style, it's in the way you make people smile. Being nice to your friends and thinking about what you say is part of what makes you cool each day."

Be Chill

"When life gets busy and your stress starts to tower, take time to relax, be sure to stop and smell the flowers."

Be Silly

"Let laughter buzz and fill the air, it's good for your health, beyond compare."

Be Happy

"Be happy like a blooming flower, spreading joy hour by hour."

Be Sad

"When you're sad, don't hide away; let tears fall like gentle rain. It's okay to feel that way; clouds make room for sun's bright rays."

Be Upset

"When you're angry and upset, it's okay, but don't forget to talk about it to ease your mind. Be honest about how you feel, letting your emotions heal."

Be a Team Player

"Teamwork makes the dream work. Together we can thrive, like bees in a hive."

Be Kind

"Spread kindness day and night,
let your joy shine bright."

Be Sweet Like Honey

"Love, oh sweet love, like the honey we make, share it freely, give and take."

Be Thankful

"Being thankful each day brings positivity and light our way."

Be Respectful

"Being respectful, kind and true, is very important especially if they are different than you."

Be Relaxed

"It's good to relax and get some rest so the next day you can be your best"

Be Sleepy

"Make sure to get enough sleep each night so you wake up feeling refreshed and bright."

but never forget to be yourself!

Made in the USA
Columbia, SC
01 September 2024